# Leadership & Youth Building Peace:

the United Nations and Nigeria's National Youth Service Corp in Perspective.

Paul Omojo Omaji

**Library of Congress Cataloguing-in-Publication entry**

Creator: Omaji, Paul, author.
Title: Leadership & Youth Building Peace: the United Nations and Nigeria's National Youth Service Corps in Perspective/Paul Omojo Omaji.

ISBN-13: 978-1978008519
ISBN-10: 1978008511

Notes: Includes bibliographical references and index.

Subjects: Leadership, Youth, Peace, United Nations, National Youth Service Corps.

*Printed by Createspace, Amazon, USA*

# DEDICATION

Youth of the World, committed to
Virtuous Leadership for Peace and
Development

# CONTENTS

The UN & Nigeria's NYSC in Perspective

# ACKNOWLEDGMENTS

Like my previous publications, this book drew much help from many, to whom I owe a depth of gratitude. Let me particularly acknowledge a few here.

- The United Nations Development Programme Office in Nigeria, which invited me to deliver a lecture at the 2017 International Youth Day commemoration it organized in conjunction with Nigeria's National Youth Service Corps.
- Professor Iliya S. Dongs of the National Open University of

Nigeria and Mr David Ojelabi of the Nigeria Security and Civil Defence Corps, who recommended me for the lecture.

- The over 2000 participants at the lecture who expressed strong love for the ideas that inspired this book.

- All those who fanned the embers of leadership, which continue to burn in me over the years and across several continents.

- My wife (Alice), our children (Ruth, Reuben, Timothy, & Tabitha) and their spouses, and our grandchildren (Cathrine, Joshua, Isaac, Elijah & Noah) from whom I continue to draw the zest for life in all that I do.

- My parents (Mr & Mrs Omaji Akwu – both now late) and siblings with whom I grew up securely to become a person embracing a worthy brand of leadership.

- The Most High Triune God - my Creator, Deliverer and Sustainer, who models the *ultimate leadership* of the persuasive and sacrificial brands highlighted in this book.

# 1

# Introduction

This publication is inspired by the public lecture I had the honour of delivering to commemorate the 2017 International Youth Day (IYD) in Nigeria, under the theme *"Youth*

*Building Peace*". The commemoration programme was organised by the United Nations Development Programme (UNDP) in conjunction with the governing agency for harnessing the elite group within the youth category in Nigeria for service, namely the National Youth Service Corps (NYSC).

Looking back over my works during most of my professional life in the academia, I notice that I've always gravitated towards matters that concern the youth: education, wellbeing services, law and justice, and active citizenship. This disposition has increased as I've ventured into the leadership question, beyond my professional discipline as a criminologist. I still haven't fully understood why.

Nevertheless, I hold this to be true that, any nation that mismanages its youth has compromised its future. Put differently, "a nation can only afford to neglect the growth and development of its youth at its own peril" (Nigeria's National Youth Policy, 2009). Or, as Irena Bokova – Director General of UNESCO - put it most recently (2017), "the development of any society depends on how well it nurtures its young women and men, how well they are supported"[1]. This is a *leadership* call.

---

[1] Irena Bokova, Message for the International Youth Day, 2017.

It is not just that the youth are almost always numerically significant or in the majority relative to the other segments of the population. There is something more potent about this age category called 'youth'. The quantum of their imagination is stupendous. So, also, is their vitality and combustible energy. Left untapped, these assets can turn into liabilities.

I learnt that human beings are

"fearfully and wonderfully made"[2].
Look no further than the youth to find
the incontrovertible evidence for this.

Thankfully, when the United Nations
(UN) system emerged after World War
II, it did not take long for it to
recognise that the dynamism of the
youth must be comprehensively
harnessed for development or the
nations of the world would
perpetually grapple with destructive

---

[2] Psalm 139: 14-16, Holy Bible.

forces. This is one area where I have admired the UN leadership: rising above several cleavages (geographical or ideological) to serve as the voice of conscience to the entire world about the youth. I can hear the voice saying: look after your youth; engage them for your constructive ventures; your destiny hangs on this!

It is therefore thrilling to see the UN and the NYSC working together[3]. Even

---

[3] Kingsley (2015) refers to the NYSC as "a pool for the most

more exciting for me, is the theme that talks about 'youth' and 'peace building' in the same breath. This is happening at such a time when the face of conflict and violence in Nigeria and most of the world is the face of the youth, going by the images in the mainstream media[4].

---

enlightened and sophisticated class of Nigerian youths who are brought periodically from diverse socio-cultural and religious backgrounds with the sole purpose of building a strong, indivisible and united Nigeria". See http://www.nairaland.com/2458540/role-corps-members-leadership-development

[4] There is a widespread belief, accentuated by media representations, that "most violent activities, ranging from armed robbery, cultism, rape, street fighting, electoral violence, to violence during crises moments in Nigeria are being perpetrated by youths", Feyisola (2013) @ http://www.antigraft.org/events/2013/jun/role-youth-

The theme is quite germane, coming next after the one of 2016 that focused on "The Road to 2030" – which was meant to show how the youth can contribute to achieving the UN Agenda for Sustainable Development Goals (SDGs) by 2030.

However, as we all know, without peace no substantive (let alone, sustainable) development is possible.

---

peacebuilding-In-our-society

In this regard, Nigeria, like many other places in the world, would attest to the fact that peace building remains the Achille's heel of its *leadership* and nationhood.

The youth who gathered in Vienna, Austria, in 1991 for the first session of the UN's World Youth Forum and proposed that the IYD be declared, showed tremendous foresight. Almost a decade later, IYD was first observed in 2000, after the UN General

Assembly had endorsed it in 1999 and proclaimed August 12 of each year as the IYD. It is indeed gratifying that we are still today celebrating that conviction-driven initiative of those visionary youth.

In the rest of this book, I will reflect on the UN's commendable intervention, through its peace and development agenda, to minimise the ambivalence that had built up around the "youth" over time and how Nigeria keyed into this intervention, as its NYSC Programme exemplifies.

Further, drawing on the UN instruments for youth development and peace, I will highlight the intricate role of today's youth (especially members of the NYSC) in the burden of peace building. Lastly, I will offer some thoughts on the toolkit the youth must carry for the business of building peace for Nigeria and humanity. The book concludes with a prayer for the youth on the

assignment of building peace.

# 2

# Ambivalence: UN to the rescue

For a long time, society has been ambivalent about the youth. Many countries that talked about the vital role of young people in their destinies, simultaneously expressed paranoia about these same youth.

Here is a classic. A highly placed politician acknowledged that the million youngsters in school were "a potential gold mine for the future" of their country; that the youth were "near and dear to the hearts" of all their citizens. Then, in the same breath, he delivered the sting of ambivalence: "...but embedded in that very same body of youngsters is the potential for harm and danger, and the commission of crime and anguish, and the victimization of themselves and others".[5]

There are countless examples of nations that do acknowledge the youth as their most 'treasured asset'. Yet, they maintain a morbid fear of the 'young' - seeing them as representing the 'risks and dangers involved in

---

[5] See Omaji, P. (2003) *Responding to Youth Crime: Towards Radical Criminal Justice Partnerships.* The Federation Press, Sydney.

everyday life'. They *idealise* the youth as "leaders of tomorrow" and, by the same token, *demonise* them as a problem group - spoilt home brats, hoodlums, idle, protesting or resisting, prone to drug and drag, given to violence and vandalism, anti-authoritarian, subversive – and inevitably criminal.

You may not know that time there was when some people wished there were no youth. Shakespeare captured this moment in his *The Winter's Tale*: "I would that there was no age between sixteen and [twenty-three], or that youth would sleep out the rest; for there is nothing in the between, but getting wenches with child, wronging the ancientry, stealing, fighting"[6].

We can see from all of this, that the logical next step after manufacturing the image of "menacing, out-of-control, armed-and-dangerous youth

---

[6] Act III, scene iii.

who are not responsible to society [and] not respectful of any authority"[7], is the criminalisation of young people.

Not surprisingly, the society hands such youth over to the criminal justice system or the army to control. A society that hangs its future on today's youth and happily sends them out to be punished or caged, is suffering from the disease of ambivalence!

---

[7] Omaji (2003), op.cit., pp18-19.

Does all this mean that the youth are passive actors in a drama in which the script is written exclusively by groups outside their age bracket? The answer is no.

Serious research shows that young people are also *producers* of, or active participants in, the images constructed about them[8]. In this role,

---

[8] See: Richards, L. (1991) "The appearance of youthful subculture: A theoretical perspective on deviance", in Thompson, W. and Bynum, J. (eds) *Juvenile Delinquency: Classic and contemporary*

young people may not have a controlling influence, but they surely have a contributory influence. They are not 'helpless dupes' of the societal constructionist machine.

As the post-modernist, Michel Foucault, once observed, 'subject populations themselves do take on an identity and participate in the

---

*readings*. Boston: Allyn and Bacon. Pp365-393; Bessant, J. (1993) *Constituting categories of youth: towards the 21st century*. Bundoora, Vic: National Centre for Socio-Legal Studies; Bessant, J.; Sercombe, H. and Watts, R. (1998) *Youth Studies: an Australian perspective*. South Melbourne: Longman; and Omaji (2003), op.cit.

development of discourses around their population group'.

In this regard, young people use subcultures as one way to forge their own category of 'youth' and its attendant images. They do this by taking on, inventing, or latching onto artefacts that express their feelings or define their stance in relation to the world in which they live.

The Hippie movement which

represented a middle and upper-class youthful subculture in the 1960s clearly illustrates this argument. It advocated active participation and self-expression rather than passive spectating in indulgent lifestyle.

Today, we have the Generation Y, otherwise known as the Millennials or 'Noughties' - defined by fashion and music, and fueled by social networking, pinging and other referral technologies.

By definition, the active nature of all such expressions almost invariably brings the youth into conflict with their world. Where the adult members of society perceive such activities as subversion (and this is how the conflict generally starts), the stage is set for an inter-generational 'war' of resistance or cultural hegemony.

It looked like it was going to be a downward spiral in that type of adult-youth mutual interaction or image construction, until the UN intervened in 1965 with the *Declaration on the Promotion among Youth of the Ideals of Peace, Mutual Respect and Understanding between Peoples.*

That intervention began to chart a new trajectory of how the world should interact with its youth. In the Declaration, we began to see the UN Members States starting to acknowledge as a matter of course that the contribution of young people

– defined as those between the ages

of 15 and 24 years[9] – is essential for

the development of society.

The youth, themselves, also began to

assert their newly recognised positive

potentialities.

Twenty years later, the UN General

Assembly proclaimed 1985 as the

---

[9] Note that, over time, different age brackets have been adopted by different countries to define who is a youth in their own individual contexts.

*International Youth Year* (IYY), with a particular focus on participation, development and peace. The first major event in that year was the World Congress on Youth, organised by UNESCO in Barcelona, Spain, July 8-15, 1985.

Significantly, the Congress issued the *Barcelona Declaration* which "recognised the profound importance of the direct participation of youth in shaping the future of humankind and the valuable contribution that youth can make to the implementation of a new international economic order based on equity and justice". It further recognised that mutual respect and understanding are "an essential instrument for achieving peace, understood not simply as the absence of war but as a prerequisite for social justice".

In its subsequent direction-setting activities, the UN has continued to drive home the need for nations to be absolutely clear about the assets they have in their youth and the strategic importance of mobilising those assets for their peace and development.

Thus, for instance, the UN General Assembly adopted *Resolution A/RES/64/134* in 2009, proclaiming the year commencing on 12 August 2010 as the *International Year of Youth: Dialogue and Mutual Understanding*. It was part of the effort to harness the energy, imagination and initiative of the world's youth in overcoming the challenges facing humankind: from enhancing peace to boosting economic development.

Little wonder, that event was used to invite governments, civil society, individuals and communities worldwide to promote the ideals of peace, freedom, progress and solidarity towards youth development and the achievement of the Millennium Development Goals which ended in 2015.

The event turned out to be a fitting end to the *International Decade for a Culture of Peace and Non-violence for the Children of the World (2001-2010)*, which the UN had proclaimed for the promotion of standards to encourage and enhance peaceful co-existence.

Since 2010, the UN system, through its Inter-Agency Network on Youth Development, has adopted the *UN Framework Approach for the International Year of Youth*. This Framework sets three strategic objectives for the IYY, all aimed at optimising the asset-value of the youth. The objectives are to:

1. create awareness: increase commitment and investment in youth;

2. mobilize and engage: increase youth participation and partnerships; and

3. connect and build bridges: increase intercultural understanding among youth.

The theme of the 2017 celebration of the IYD derived directly from the UN Security Council *Resolution 2250,* adopted in December 2015. The Resolution did set a global framework for youth to engage in peacebuilding.

But, here is the aspect of the Resolution that underscores the focus of this section of the book.

The Resolution emphasised the UN system's commitment to transforming the normative understanding of youth from victims and/or perpetrators of violence and conflict, to focusing on the positive roles that the youth can and should play in peacebuilding and conflict prevention[10].

---

[10] See UNDP (2017) "Concept Note – International Youth Day

On the whole, the UN's coming to the rescue in a world that was inexorably ambivalent about the youth is among the best things that the world has witnessed since the mid-20$^{th}$ century. The inherent leadership is praiseworthy and exemplary.


Today, only recalcitrant governments, bent on destroying themselves and their countries, can continue to

_______________

2017".

harbour the negative stereotyping or reckless disempowerment of their youth. Such stance can no longer reasonably subsist after the UN direction-setting interventions since the 1960s.

# 3

# Nigeria and its youth: the NYSC example

Notwithstanding that vestiges of the negative stereotyping of the youth show up from time to time, Nigeria has by and large taken after the UN leadership in the progressive imaging of the youth. Thus, we can find in Nigeria's national youth policy such expressions as the following:

> Youth are one of the greatest assets that any nation can have. Not only are they legitimately regarded as the future leaders, they are potentially and actually the greatest investment for a country's development. [They are] recognized as a vital resource whose future prospects

are inextricably tied to that of their country. They are the valued possession of any nation or region. Without them there can be no future. They are the center of reconstruction and development[11].

Further, there have been several institutional platforms that Nigeria has established, or proposed, to foster

---

[11] See the *Second National Youth Policy Document of the Federal Republic of Nigeria 2009.*

youth development since it got Independence in 1960. These platforms include:

- the Citizen and Leadership Training Centre Nigeria. The Centre was given a legal status in 1960 and modified by a decree in 1989 with the mandate of leadership training, empowerment, and character development among young people in the country;

- the National Youth Council of

Nigeria (NYCN), founded in 1964 to be the voice and the umbrella organization for youth organizations in the country;

- the setting up of the Federal Ministry of Youth and Sports in the 1970s;

- the NYSC, established by Decree in 1973; and

- the National Youth Development Council (proposed in 2009).

To date, the NYSC Programme stands as the most prominent demonstration that Nigeria has recognised the value of its youth for peace and development. The Programme was established in furtherance, generally, of the Federal Government post-war *Policy of Reconstruction, Rehabilitation and Reconciliation.*

Its design focused on raising a new corps of highly disciplined and detribalized Nigerian youth. The goal was primarily to promote the 'reconciliation' leg (national unity) of the Policy by affording the youth the opportunity of service to communities other than their own.

The hope has been that the participating youth would "develop a sense of corporate existence and common destiny of the people of Nigeria"[12]. Such youth would arise from, among other things, being

---

[12] See *NYSC Handbook*, 1995)

"exposed to modes of living of the people in different parts of the country, with a view to removing prejudices, eliminating ignorance and confirming at first hand the similarities among Nigerians of all ethnic groups"[13].

The NYSC is the longest surviving government programme in Nigeria - with the utmost purpose of ensuring

---

[13] One of the objectives [d(iii)] enunciated in the NYSC legislation.

unity and peace in the country. And, it is unique in its emphasis on inculcating in Nigerian youth at least two core leadership capabilities. One, the spirit of selfless service to the community. And, two, and the spirit of oneness and brotherhood of all Nigerians, as well as facilitating national integration irrespective of cultural or social background[14].

---

[14] "Building and Sustaining peace and security in multiethnic Nigeria", at
https://dlc.dlib.indiana.edu/dlc/bitstream/handle/10535/939
7/WG26_Okotoni%2C%20Olu.pdf?sequence=1&isAllowed=y

Of course, there are debates about the extent to which NYSC has been successful vis-à-vis its laudable objectives. There are strong voices on both sides of these debates[15].

Nevertheless, considering that the ideals for which the NYSC was established are still valid in Nigeria

---

[15] For example, there are reports that President Jonathan and Alhaji Abubakar Sa'ad (Sultan of Sokoto) consider it a success that should retained and strengthened; and there are reports that Oluwole Aluko, an Ibadan-based lawyer and Imo State Governor, Chief Rochas Okorocha have called for the scrapping of the the Scheme – because it amounts to servitude and forced labour; and is therefore inconsistent with the 1999 Constitution or that it has outlived its usefulness by failing to promote unity.

today, and bearing in mind that there is hardly any other formal institutional platform that can rival its position in contemporary Nigeria, it was right that the UN chose the NYSC as the strategic partner for the 2017 IYD commemoration. That move clearly recognised the NYSC's strategic and critical contributions towards "youth building peace".

# 4

# Youth and the burden of peace building

Peace building, in its basic rendition, is an intervention that is designed to prevent the start or resumption of conflict or violence. It involves addressing the root causes, creating a societal expectation for peaceful coexistence or conflict resolution, and stabilising society, politically and socio-economically.

In contradistinction to peace-enforcement and peace-keeping, peace-building is essentially a preventative project. It ensures the populace have freedom from fear (negative peace), freedom from want (positive peace) and freedom from humiliation arising from conflict or violence[16]. A core *leadership* role!

In Nigeria, and several parts of the world, such intervention remains a very daunting project. Nearly 60 years after Independence, Nigeria continues to witness forces that are generally antithetical to peace. These forces include:

- tribal and ethnic affinity or allegiances;

---

[16] Adapted from https://en.wikipedia.org/wiki/Peacebuilding

- bad leadership;

- militarised culture;

- large scale corruption;

- institutional failure;

- poverty;

- religious extremism;

- inequitable management of resources;

- deplorable conditions of social and infrastructural amenities;

- unemployment/under-employment/unemployability;

- struggling security agents or institutions; and

- porous border entry points.

The self-help manner in which Nigerians deploy several ethnic, cultural and militia movements[17] in the vortex of these varied forces, has

---

[17] Including the Bakassi Boys, O'Odua Peoples Congress (OPC), Movement of the Actualization of the Sovereign State of Biafra (MASSOB), Movement for the Survival of the Ogoni People (MOSOP), Arewa People Congress (APC), O'Odua Liberation Movement (OLM), Revolutionary Council of Nigeria (RCN), Igbo Peoples Congress (IPC), Ijaw Youth Congress (IYC), Ijaw National Congress, the Hisbah groups, Egbesu Boys, Niger Delta People Volunteer Force (NDPVF) and and more recently the Boko Haram terrorism in the North East.

complicated and deepened the burden of peace building for any conceivable interventions. These movements have proved very challenging to Nigeria's leadership in all jurisdictions (local, state and federal), in terms of defeating them or aligning them with the national interest of peace in Nigeria.

Consequently, Nigeria continues to grapple with numerous human rights abuses from their activities in a manner that renders peace quite fragile. These abuses include kidnapping, armed robbery, clashes, rape, extortions, murder, and a general sense of insecurity[18]. Significantly, the political apparatus seems overwhelmed.

The fact of the matter is that, apart from the NYSC and the Amnesty Programmes (of recent pedigree) , most of the formal institutional

---

[18] See Okotoni and Awotokun (2014) op.cit.

approaches to building peace in Nigeria to date have failed to make any substantive dent on security and safety challenges in the country[19]. This is, perhaps, why the country is still looking up to the NYSC with a renewed optimism that its participating youth would help build peace in the land.

The Amnesty Programme, we may

---

[19] For example, the 1999 Truth Commission (Justice Oputa Panel) was a non-starter; the State of emergency declarations (2004; 2013) were largely unsuccessful; and the last National Conference (2014) is still out there with the jury.

recall, started in 2009 when the Nigerian President, Alhaji Umaru Musa Yar'Adua GCFR, proclaimed a 60-day unconditional amnesty period on June 25, 2009 for militants in the Niger Delta. He did this, as a step towards resolving the protracted insecurity in the region.

The terms of the Amnesty include the willingness and readiness of militants to surrender their arms, unconditionally renounce militancy and sign an undertaking to this effect. In return, the government pledged its commitment to institute programmes to assist their disarmament, demobilization, rehabilitation and provision of reintegration assistance to the militants[20].

The country has maintained its commitment to this Programme. However, the 'peace-impact' and

[20] See the Office of the Special Adviser to the President on the Niger Delta at http://www.osapnd.gov.ng/index/ndap.

'national integration effect' of the programme is a subject for another painstaking study.

Regarding the renewed optimism for the NYSC, some prominent voices have been talking up the role of the Scheme – especially against the backdrop of the incessant agitation for restructuring, which is interpreted by some Nigerians as a call for fracturing Nigeria or even plunging it into war.

For instance, the NYSC Director General, Brigadier General Kazaure, stated during one of his visits in 2017 to the Enugu Camp of the Scheme that "NYSC is all about Nigerian unity and national integration. We should love ourselves, work together as a team and make Nigeria united. We should make sure that Nigeria remains one entity"[21].

---

[21] https://www.vanguardngr.com/2017/08/ensure-nigeria-remains-one-entity-nysc-dg-tells-corps-members/.

President Buhari reinforced this expectation in September 2017. Speaking to newsmen at his country home after the Eid-el-Kabir prayers, he said that the NYSC scheme had over the years continued to pursue the purpose of integrating the country. In particular, he noted that the diversity of cultures remained Nigeria's greatest strength and that, with the Scheme, the dream of a unified Nigeria remained a reality[22].

---

[22] https://www.vanguardngr.com/2017/09/sallah-read-buhari-told-corps-members-visited-daura/.

Considering that the perpetrators and victims in Nigeria's state of non-peace are predominantly young, Irena Bokova indeed hit the nail on the head when she said: "young people carry the heaviest burdens of conflict and violence - they are also essential for any lasting solution leading to peace"[23].


The question is, can the current

---

[23] See her message for the IYD 2017, op.cit.

participating youth deliver on this optimism? Or, is Nigeria (and other countries that hold such hope) misguided in their expectations? To appreciate the significance of the burden that the expectations place on the youth, let me reiterate my earlier point about today's youth who are said to belong to the "Generation Y".

Given the chronological delineations of generations (since the 1800s), and the fact that Nigeria labels persons of

18-35 years as youth[24], most of the NYSC members today are in the 'Generation Y' cohort, presumably born within the 1980-2000 bracket. So, they are the Millennials, also known as the Noughties, Digital Natives (Internet generation, iGen and/or the Net generation), Generation Me, Generation Rent and Echo Boomers.

---

[24] This differs from the UN definition of 15-24 years, but the upper limit is consistent with 15-35years in the African Youth Charter, 2006.

If you concentrate on the mainstream media, you would confront a picture of the Millennials as lazy, narcissistic, impatient, 'we want it now' or instantly self-gratifying, and entitled selfie-lovers[25].

Were this to be the end of discussion, most of the persons who believe in the place of the youth in peace building would sink into despondency. The reason is that,

---

[25] See http://luckyattitude.co.uk/millennial-characteristics/

there is no way such a youth group - massive in size and most likely to dominate everything for years to come - can be an asset in peace building in Nigeria or elsewhere for that matter!

Thankfully, though, there is another side to the Millennials that we must explore; and this is where my hope lies. They see themselves, and have been found, to a large extent, to be the most:

- technologically savvy (constantly connected to the world – hopefully not all for fun and games or keeping up with social contacts but for research and education);

- civic-oriented - with a strong sense of community, both on local and global scale, focusing on larger societal needs rather than individual needs, believing in the value of political engagement with the conviction that government can be a powerful force for good, and feeling obligated to do their part to make the world a better place;

- conscious on health, social, economic and environmental issues - willing to pay extra for sustainable offerings with the belief that it can influence the world with the power of the wallet (or credit card), embracing the differences in one another (respecting and valuing diversity) as global citizens who have a responsibility to make the world a more equitable and sustainable place;

- entrepreneurial - startup kids who grew up on entrepreneurship watching Steve Jobs lead the renewed Apple, Mark Zuckerberg create a social media sensation and other young innovators disrupt traditional industries; and

- compassionate and progressive - volunteering to help, change and improve other people's lives with a bit of disdain for selfishness, rejecting the status quo, willing to challenge the system if there is something they could improve on, and wanting to move the country forward, to advocate change, to advance new ideas and policies[26].

In this latter characterisation, we can see certain qualities that (if properly harnessed, as I will show in the next Chapter) would position today's youth to effectively take on the peace building assignment, no matter how heavy or daunting it may seem.

---

[26] Ibid.

If the previous generations lacked serious political will to take decisive actions on crucial matters affecting the country' s peace and security, I would like to believe that today's youth as here characterised will act differently.

Where overpoliticisation of almost every issue (social, economic, ethnic, cultural and religious) has done great damage to the unity and stability of nations, I see today's youth challenging that status quo.

Where amplified corruption has been killing nations (as Nigeria exemplifies), I see that today's youth will muster genuine national interest to overturn personal, ethnic, religious and regional feeders of corruption.

And, where institutional atrophy - through leadership and management failures, has held down nations' progress toward peace, I see today's youth undertaking the necessary comprehensive and rigorous reforms that will produce strong institutions (not just "strong men") to get such nations back up on the path to their manifest destinies of peace.

Clearly, this burden is weighty. However, if there is any cause in nations today worthy of all the powerful assets we have in the youth, it is that of peace building. And, despite the many challenges and distortions to the original intent of the *UN Framework Approach for the International Year of Youth* and the NYSC scheme in Nigeria, I am optimistic that today's participating youth still constitute one of the best instruments of any peace building project.

# 5

# Toolkit for youth peace building

No worker goes to work without the necessary toolkit. Similarly, it is counterintuitive for any youth to take up peace building without being properly equipped. There are so many tools I can list for the youth to have in their toolkit for this assignment.

However, I am a strong believer in the saying that everything rises, stands and falls on leadership. Therefore, the one tool I would seriously recommend for youth's toolkit for peace building is to sharpen their leadership capability.

As you may be aware, the leadership

question has vexed many aspects of human life. Not everyone who occupies a position or parades the corridor of power is a leader! Certainly not those who steal, kill and destroy the commonwealth for whatever reason, including the pursuit of their selfish interests. This begs the question of what leadership actually means.

Google 'leadership' now and you'll get over 150 million entries. Also, there are now about 400,000 books on this subject. Stack all of these books on each other, assuming each is about one inch thick, and you'll get a stack of over 33,000 feet high. That would be taller than Mt Everest![27] So, we need to be clear as to what I am here asking the youth to do.

Let me cut to the chase. Leadership is influence, but not all influence is

---

[27] See Clarke, T. (2009) *The Leadership Test: Will You Pass?*. Oxonian Press, Utah, USA.

leadership[28]. You can resort to a coercive influence or deceptive (manipulative) influence. Your behaviour in each of these two moulds would be autocratic or ambivalent. But you will not go far in your peace building assignment with that style.

In fact, such behaviour will take you out of the spirit and ambit of the UN

---

[28] Omaji, P. (2015) *Audacity of Leading Right: An Odyssey Towards Virtuous Leadership*. Createspace, Amazon, Charleston, USA.

and the NYSC, which are designed among other things to raise the moral tone of the world, in general, and the youth building peace in particular. There is no morality in coercion or deception.

As a former UN Secretary General once said, a successful peace building process must be inclusive and transformative[29], not alienational or

---

[29] See the UN Secretary-General's (2012) *Report on Peacebuilding in the Aftermath of Conflict*.

transactional - which is what you get from the coercive and deceptive forms of influence[30]. From all my personal and professional experiences to date, I have come to the view that only persuasive (authentic) and sacrificial (virtuous) forms of influence can guarantee the outcome that the UN Secretary General talked about.

These forms of influence would enable the youth to "make the right

—————————————————————

[30] Omaji, P. (2015) op.cit.

things happen, in the right way, at the right time and for the right reasons"[31]. They would predispose the youth to:

- possess bias towards building peaceful communities;

- display a can-do and do-it-well mindset in the quest for sustainable peace;

- be driven by result- or impact- focus in preventing and

---

[31] I am constantly working to simplify the definition of leadership. This is the one I formulated recently, See Omaji, P. (2017) "Leadership and Decision-making", a leadership development workshop for senior management of Nigeria Deposit Insurance Commission, 8 August 2017.

resolving conflict, violence and extremism; and

- model moral excellence - with a high sense of integrity in all their civic engagement and active citizenship.

It wouldn't matter which approach the location of the youth requires them to take towards peace building. Whether it is:

- the human rights approach where the youth sensitise the

community to the international standards for peaceful coexistence;

- the economic approach where they promote access to opportunities for development;

- the socio-political approach where they help to connect people to civil society, political arena, and participation in public life; or

- the sociocultural approach where they foster intra-youth

and intergenerational dialogue and understanding.

A leadership capability, grounded in the persuasive and sacrificial forms of influence, will make the youth excel unashamedly as peace builders any day, anywhere.

It takes leadership of this type to muster political will for constructive work in nations. Today's youth must make a 180° turn away from the way of the wayward, coercive, deceptive and exploitative political class and reposition their nations for peace and prosperity.

Today's youth must prove to be leaders by denouncing ethno-religious politics and embracing development-oriented national politics, while engaging intelligently with the global community.

These youth must shun the

perception and practice of corruption; they must govern as exemplars of integrity without which, peace and development are impossible.

Today's youth must (re) introduce dynamic and upright leadership and management of nations. In this regard, their focus must be on building and/or strengthening institutions, while frowning with passion on the 'big man' syndrome.

The ensuing institutions must enthrone a national philosophy of "right is might" (Omaji 2017b)[32]. They must deploy the philosophy as a contextual pre-condition for active citizenship and all engagements for peace and development.

Herein lies the call of the youth to leadership in peace building. All nations, particularly those still

---

[32] Omaji, P. (2017b) "The Accountable Organisation: Personal and Organisational Accountability", Leadership Workshop for the Senior Executives of the NNPC Medical Services Ltd. 13 October 2017. Abuja.

grappling with peace and development challenges (Nigeria being a glaring example), need their youth to step up to the plate. For these nations, the need to 'make the right things happen, in the right way, at the right time and for the right reasons' is imperative and urgent.

# 6

# Conclusion: nobility in the UN, NYSC and the Youth

Peace building is a task that must be done in the entire world. It is most noble that the UN system uses the IYD to constantly remind the world to value, and to look to, its youth as the best agent to carry out this task. In Nigeria, there is no better instrument than the NYSC (mobilising the elite youth group) with which to effectively pursue this daunting task.

While certain mannerisms of today's youth, as the Millennials, may be counterproductive to this project, the preponderance of their empowering characteristics suggests that they really can be counted upon to take peace building to a greater height. For those youth who think their lives to date do not position them for peace building, I say it is not too late to do something about it now. Even if they have been manufacturers of weapons of war or merchants of death, they can still turn around.

Alfred Nobel, a Swedish inventor and businessman, did so! By age 30, he had already acquired several patents for his inventions on how to prepare gunpowder and detonators. When serendipity confronted him with what the world thought about his invention of dynamites, he changed to become a philanthropist.

After reading a <u>premature obituary</u> which condemned him for profiting from the sales of arms, Nobel bequeathed his fortune to establish five <u>prizes</u> in order to leave a better legacy after his real death. One of those prices is the Noble Peace Prize!

My dear young people, regardless of your background, the greatest legacy you can bequeath to peace building and become worthy ambassadors of the UN and NYSC peace projects, will come from you becoming  persuasive and sacrificial leaders. Use your youth time to hone, or lay a solid foundation for, this ultimate (virtuous) leadership. Your environment may not encourage you to carry forward this revolutionary destiny for the world.

Who can forget the wanton killing of some NYSC members, in the course of discharging their leadership duty, during the post-2011 election violence in Nigeria?[33] Sadly, the youth of the world may not completely escape the harm's way while carrying

---

[33] Alubo, O. and Umar, M. (2011), in their article: "Nigeria and the Challenge of National Integration", observed that some NYSC members who served as INEC ad hoc staff were attacked and 10 were killed in Bauchi State. See Maduagwu, M.; Akpuru-Aja, A.; Jumare, I.; and Para-Mallam, O. (eds) *Nigeria's 50 Years of Nation-Building: Stock-Taking and Looking Ahead*. National Institute for Policy and Strategic Studies, Kuru, Jos.

out the noble universal duty of peace building.

However, with the "imagination and drive of the young, tamed by discipline and commitment"[34] for all things constructive as outlined in the penultimate Chapter above, you can attain this consciousness of leadership and build peace from where you are – if need be, sacrificially. As Nelson

---

[34] Martin Luther King (1961) "The Time for Freedom has Come" in Washington, J. (1986) *A Testament of Hope: the Essential Writings and Speeches of Martin Luther King Jr.* Harper Collins Publishers, New York.

Mandela once said, "it always seems impossible until it's done".

The youth cannot afford to, and they will not, disappoint their world. Hence, I wholeheartedly offer this prayer for them:

Oh God of creation, direct their noble cause. Guide the youth (in the UN and NYSC systems) right. Help them the truth to know; in love and honesty to grow. And living just and true; great lofty heights attain. To build, uprightly and timely, a world where peace and justice shall reign[35]. Amen.


Then, and only then, the UN, the NYSC and the youth of the world would have converged in the noblest display of *leadership*, namely: "making the right things happen, in the right way, at the right time and for the right reasons" (Omaji 2017 op. cit).

---

[35] Adapted from the second stanza of Nigeria's National Anthem.

# ABOUT THE AUTHOR

Paul Omojo Omaji is a Professor of Criminology and Vice Chancellor Emeritus. He trained in Sociology, Criminology, and Law in Nigeria and Australia. He has researched, published and lectured in these fields for about 36 years across Nigeria, Australia, Singapore, India, South Africa, the US, Canada, UK, and Sweden.

In the area of leadership, Professor Omaji has had over 40 years of community and professional experiences. These include Senior Executive positions in the Australian Government public service. In these positions, he provided policy advice at federal ministerial levels. He also led his teams to successfully deliver government programmes.

These programmes were implemented in local communities and overseas countries, including the US, UK, Sweden, Denmark, Austria, the Czech Republic, Italy, and France.

Professor Omaji's journey in the

academia took him through all the levels in the university administration, culminating in his appointment as the pioneer Vice Chancellor of a private University in Nigeria.

Building on these cumulative experiences and exposures, Professor Omaji has taken up consultancy and training in leadership and management development under *Omaji Leadership Solutions* and the *Virtuous Leaders Development Network*, where he currently serves as the Chief Executive Officer.

Aside from his disciplinary works, Professor Omaji has published some leadership capacity-building books including:

- *Audacity of Leading Right: An Odyssey Towards Virtuous Leadership;*

- *Lead For Life: 7 Essentials of Upright & High-Impact Leadership;* and

- *Melody Lines of a Christian Leader Selected Weekly Wisdom of Reverend Benson Reuben.*

# INDEX

## B



## C



## D



## E



## F



## G